A Love Letter to Say
There Is No Love

by

Maria Williams-Russell

FutureCycle Press
futurecycle.org

A Love Letter to Say There Is No Love

Published by FutureCycle Press
Cave Spring, Georgia, U.S.A.

ISBN: 978-0-9828612-0-2

Contents

Nests in the Rafters

The neighbor's mother died
in the backyard beside the wire fence.
A black procession
threads between our windows.
I remember her thick shoes, her chest
swelled to meet her mouth,
the sun like a pistol shot that morning.
They found her with a mouse
caught in her rigored hand,
the dog barking by her body.
She was fond of you, the neighbor said,
who thinks it's spring has brought the hives.
We had the fence, I sigh.
I didn't say how nights were busy
stitching through the windows
something like a rope of bees.

Carrying Water

Imagine if before war, we grew armor.
Before a storm, fins.
Last night, the seeds on the sill grew
into windmills.
My babies climbed to the top
and were immediately tossed.
I spent the morning picking what fell.
Follow me. Somewhere
near the rubble is a twine-thin creek.
If I could, I would grow gills
the way a driver grows wings
before she slams into a tree.
We could wet our lips.
We could bring a small drop back.

Last Night the Fan Whirred in the Window

I must have gotten up to take a drink because

this morning the faucet was running

and two moths spun like forget-me-nots

in the drain.

                    I dreamt of fallen dancers'

still pointed toes littering a stage,

tutus billowing even though.

And I there

busily carving caskets out of theater seats,

sewing little head pillows

with my hair.

Games We Play

We twirl like ash past the flue,
shimmy-shake and do the bump
beside the stove.
The children sing kettle songs—
I wish I were an engine,
I wish I were a crow.
The neighbors' curtains close.
Around, around we go.
Then we wrap our bodies tight in wool,
crawl inside the cupboards singing—
We are not cold.

Without Shepherds

Across the field,
a young woman spins wool.
I wonder how her hands hold up.

Last we met,
she said her father died,
had gone outside and gotten hit by a truck.

Also, the colors for wool
these days depress her, the neon blues,
the fuchsia pinks.
Nothing real, she said.

The Way I Remember

You once said a deer's hoof reminded you of a bedpost.
 A frog's skin was a lullaby.
You said when the flower beds were full with root
we could bury our savings there.
I have been digging.
You of course are gone. Under my bedside table
I have gathered all the spoons from my thoughts;
the ones that ladled you still shine. That is why
I keep a collection of lily pads in my head
and count the hoof prints in the garden after a full moon.

Before the Storm

We are passing Antelope Hill.
There is no such thing
but we hear scraping horns
and anxious hoof steps on cold
and we know all about it.
Our own hands are stuffed into pockets
and we see each other's breath.
Of course, it is gray
and there will be no moon.

Of course, it is gray
and there will be no moon.
Our own hands are stuffed into pockets
and we see each other's breath.
We hear scraping horns
and anxious hoof steps on cold
and we know all about it.
There is no such thing but
we are passing Antelope Hill.

How We Live

War sits across from me in the tub.
He has not said a word, but fountains
spit through his blurred teeth
and that incessant dark grinning
make it impossible to read.
I always retreat, place the damp page
between me and cracks in the porcelain.
Or slip beneath to listen for intruders in the pipes.
We are married many long years now.
He has seen me shiver and pace
and raise a knife against his camouflage.
Some days, it feels he might tire of me
and then I am even more a widow.
Other days, I think he pours my tea.

Morning Prayer

Cartoons have taken over the house.
The children and I avoid
the bombs and dropping anvils
by wishing for a pet.
We are singular in our dream
and disappear inside the mayhem
by believing we are rubber
chew toys or long balls of yarn.
We have even dared go as far
as to sneak a small dish outside the door.
Dear Lord, send a bird for me
and for the children
something with a broad back.
If anything comes,
let it know we bleed.

Tending the Hives

Other years, I kept a bat house
near the eaves, I filled the window boxes
with embers. The children slept
upside down by knees. Blood was honey then
and bees kept us a family. We and the world,
even the bats, who all eventually died
atop the coals.

I Will Never Leave You

The contractors come to seal the house
with me in it, I think,
as if I am already underground.
It has been a black winter
but now a crocus
is budding near the south foundation.
I wonder how
a woman becomes abandoned freight
or the last bit on carcass ribs.
I believe the endless snow was due
to my crouching against it.
So when the men walk through the house,
I pretend my body is the frame
and they a flock of birds
caught for a moment in the rafters.
Next year will be different, they say.
But their words are stale crumbs of air.
When the men go, I pry out
silicone foam from the basement walls
with my sharpest kitchen knife.
I sing what I believe is old:
shovel to soil,
prisoner to cement.
How slow the world is.
If only hope was a house.

A Love Letter to Say There Is No Love

I dream about fog, the black
    arrows of geese overhead.

I crawl outside my bones in sleep
    to love another and another and another.

The moon weaves blue wool
    between our lungs. We are strung.

And when I wake, the sun beats
    like a farmer on his oxen.

Winner

I look at the sun and begin to fight.
How the mouse you killed
stinks now. How
so much hair is stuck in the carpet.
We'll have to go out in the yard and wear shorts.
The neighbors start their mowers.
The ice cream truck
creeps the street. I have been
cutting hedges in my head for weeks.
A little off the top. A little more.
I am at the stumps
before the shot goes off.

Wedding Vow

I want turbine engines
and a galaxy of bullets
on my honeymoon,

machine guns and you
to sing for the dead
with, love.

You be bow,
I'll be arrow
in the silver-heavy night

and we will fight
and dream as lovers do, dream
ourselves across the dunes.

I'll become mother
and you will cup blood,
husband of war.

We will weave
our flesh into
an indestructible net.

And after that, years,
fences and the dark
clanking of soup bowls.

Together we will die
in the open corners of our lives
empty bags of skin.

My love, if not this
why be made
of dirt and spit at all.

The Leopard and the Shovel

Say there are two things— a leopard and a shovel.
The leopard is the chaser
while the shovel desperately hops
on its one handle through the old house.
Here there are several outcomes:
The leopard pounces, after a few
rounds up and down the stairs,
to find nothing but iron and wood to rub its teeth on.
Or the shovel turns to face the leopard
in a moment of deep anguish
and drops its heavy head, crushing
the leopard's skull.
Or maybe, they both get bored and walk away.
What if the shovel is love,
the leopard dreaming?
The leopard with her sleek and eyes can never
really know the shovel,
only that there is reason to chase it.
And the shovel so chased by dreaming
can never do its job of digging.
Perhaps I will set fire to the house and watch them
negotiate among the flames.

Ghosts Passing

Yesterday, I heard singing
in the old orchard.
Or is that how I forget?
A loose root
howling like a cat.

Ask Me How I Am

The bulldozers are back
and the rain. It's the neighbor's
dog who howls and rubs
herself against the fence. A protestor
killed by a bulldozer locked her knees
like wires splitting a field.
I saw it on TV. At night I dream
oil and lug nut shining
across the interstate. Tufts of hair
lie wet in the yard.

When It Comes to Pass

Eventually, there will be water,
a pool perhaps, a pond.
We will go and drink
with our lean appendages and missing hair.
Too tired to fight, we will act
as if nothing but a rough night kept us
swinging our guns and acting like maniacs.

After Long Silences

I feel it in the house too—
the long panels cover the old wood
which covers the forgotten frame.

Anyway
we are all children and not to blame,
he who is attacker
and she who is raped.

Even the sky is a green screen
stretched over a web of pipe.

Silence and Machine

I was thinking of dust
and drives along turning roads
lined with tall grass.
Of the grass's grace
as if there lived laughter in winding
mazes of stalks.
Then to dust again and curl
as a leaf toward a yellow river.
Brittled veins and road.
I am not sad.
Some inventions long all by themselves.
A body longs rest
like car and road long a kind of stopping.
And why not think years could break
like birds from branches?
Knees buckle like asphalt
and I wish for things more brilliant than me.
To wrap myself, for instance,
as if around a tree.

As Night Comes

A young man comes to the door
begging sugar and corn. The children
hide behind the furnace.
Used to be children went door to door
and night smiled curiously and brisk.
The young man shoulders the door,
raises his hands cupped for communion.
Used to be we'd have ID cards
to prove who we are— mother, beggar.
Now the blink of an eye,
the jut of a shoulder.
We are animals again, curiously
waiting for death.
Should I take off my mask, he says,
and come in?

Mettle

We are sewn
by handful and by sift.
Bits of bone and carry.
Along the river
we find ourselves
half-buried.

Acknowledgments

"Carrying Water," "Last Night the Fan Whirred in the Window,"
and "Before the Storm" are soon to be published in *Bateau*.

"Ask Me How I Am" was published in *Chronogram*.

*Book design: Cover art by Jill Battaglia, (jillbattaglia@hotmail.com);
cover design by Diane Kistner (dkistner@futurecycle.org); typeface
selection, Centaur, by the author (mariawilliams@gmail.com).*

The FutureCycle Poetry Book Prize

FutureCycle Press conducts an annual full-length poetry book competition open to any poet writing in the English language. The winning manuscript is normally published over the summer, with the poet receiving a $1,000 prize plus 25 copies of the published book. Finalists may also be offered publishing contracts. Submissions of book manuscripts are accepted from January 1 to March 31 each year for that year's prize. The press also publishes individual poems in its online magazine, *FutureCycle Poetry.* These poems, which remain online indefinitely, are collected into an annual print edition each November.

To be considered, all submissions must be received via our online submission form. To avoid unnecessary delays or unread returns of submitted work, poets should review our guidelines:

www.futurecycle.org/guidelines.aspx

Poetry Books
from FutureCycle Press

FutureCycle Poetry Book Prize Winners

Stealing Hymnals from the Choir by Timothy Martin (2010)
No Loneliness by Temple Cone (2009)

FutureCycle Poetry Book Prize Finalists

Castaway by Katherine Riegel (2010 Finalist)
Simple Weight by Tania Runyan (2010 Finalist)
Luminous Dream by Wally Swist (2010 Finalist)
Beyond the Bones by Neil Carpathios (2009 Finalist)

Full-length Books

The Porous Desert by David Chorlton
Violet Transparent by Anne Coray

Chapbooks

Colma by John Laue
Scything by Joanne Lowery
A Love Letter to Say There Is No Love by Maria Russell-Williams

www.ingramcontent.com/pod-product-compliance
Lightning Source LLC
Chambersburg PA
CBHW070357130626
46556CB00007B/3196